How to Impress a Girl

A Guide to Getting the Girl of Your Dreams

by Becca Lang

Table of Contents

Introduction 1

Chapter 1: Grooming Basics 7

Chapter 2: Preparing for the Approach 11

Chapter 3: Starting a Conversation 15

Chapter 4: Using the Internet to Your Advantage ... 21

Chapter 5: Planning an Unforgettable First Date 27

Chapter 6: Advancing to a Relationship 33

Conclusion 37

Introduction

You see a beautiful woman from across the room. You want to approach her, but you fear she is out of your league. You have found yourself in similar situations before, and each time, your introductions have ended in disaster. You will need to get into the right frame of mind this time before you walk over to introduce yourself, or it will not end any differently than before.

Think back to your previous attempts at meeting women. Did you succeed or fail miserably? What approach did you take those times when you were able to get past the introduction and actually secure a first date? Maybe it was a failed attempt to start a conversation. Can you figure out where you went wrong?

Break down the steps to your approach: You spot an attractive woman entering the room. Now, you need to figure out if you want to take a chance with her. Do you have the confidence to make that first move? Try to come up with something to say. Does your mind go blank and you fear you will become tongue tied when you start to speak?

There are three common scenarios where men's attempts at introducing themselves to women often end in failure:

First Scenario: You walk up to the beautiful woman and make a completely awkward statement which creates an extremely awkward situation. You realize right away that there is no mutual attraction, and you walk away with your figurative tail between your legs.

Second Scenario: You walk up to the beautiful woman in an attempt to impress her, and you make yourself look like an idiot. In turn, you get angry with her when she walks away from you, making you look even more like a baboon.

Third Scenario: You walk up to this beautiful woman and start acting like a cocky fool. She is not impressed, and immediately turns you down.

In each of these three scenarios, the man has to be commended for having the courage to go up and introduce himself, although he certainly will benefit from brushing up on his style.

What could have been done differently to achieve a better outcome? Have you fallen into the trap of using one of the above attempts? Do not let yourself become that clueless man at the bar or at the next party you attend. Think through the steps you took, and try to do the opposite. By changing your thought process when you find yourself attracted to a beautiful woman, you will be one step closer to finding the woman of your dreams.

© Copyright 2014 by Miafn LLC - All rights reserved.

This document is geared towards providing reliable information in regards to the topic and issue covered. The publication is sold with the idea that the publisher is not required to render accounting, officially permitted, or otherwise, qualified services. If advice is necessary, legal or professional, a practiced individual in the profession should be ordered.

- From a Declaration of Principles which was accepted and approved equally by a Committee of the American Bar Association and a Committee of Publishers and Associations.

In no way is it legal to reproduce, duplicate, or transmit any part of this document in either electronic means or in printed format. Recording of this publication is strictly prohibited and any storage of this document is not allowed unless with written permission from the publisher. All rights reserved.

The information provided herein is stated to be truthful and consistent, in that any liability, in terms of inattention or otherwise, by any usage or abuse of any policies, processes, or directions contained within is solely and completely the responsibility of the recipient reader. Under no circumstances will any legal responsibility or blame be held against the publisher for any reparation, damages, or monetary loss due to the information herein, either directly or indirectly.

Respective authors own all copyrights not held by the publisher.

The information herein is offered for informational purposes solely, and is universal as so. The presentation of the information is without contract or any type of guarantee assurance.

The trademarks that are used are without any consent, and the publication of the trademark is without permission or backing by the trademark owner. All trademarks and brands within this book are for clarifying purposes only and are the owned by the owners themselves, not affiliated with this document.

Chapter 1: Grooming Basics

Before you head out for the evening, you need to figure out what not to do when approaching a woman. Take a good look in the mirror and make sure you are presenting the best "you" possible. When presenting yourself to the possible woman of your dreams, you want her to like you for you.

Clothing and Style

Women do take notice of what you are wearing. They may not stare at the labels and judge you based on which designer you are wearing, but they definitely care if you put some thought into your wardrobe. There is a big difference between a man who has a neat and orderly sense of fashion, and a man who does not care about what he is wearing. A well-dressed man does not always have a beautiful woman by his side by default, but a bit of fashion sense does help when it comes to landing that first date.

If your style is awkward or careless, it really is not much of a style. In the eyes of a woman, an unkempt man is a lazy man. The woman you are trying to impress could reason that if you cannot put the time and thought into creating a look, you will likely not put in the time and effort needed for other things, like developing a meaningful relationship. She will not waste her time with someone who cannot spend time on themselves.

You do not need to go out and buy fancy designer clothing. If money is tight, you can find great deals on clearance racks, or even at your local thrift shop. As long as your clothing is clean and wrinkle-free and fits well, that is all that matters. Sometimes, something as simple as choosing the right clothes will help you land that first date.

Grooming and Hygiene

Now that you have taken inventory of your wardrobe and are putting your best foot forward, assess your personal hygiene habits. A beautiful woman will not be attracted to someone with messy hair, dirty teeth, or bad breath. When you are looking to impress a girl, hygiene needs to become your main priority. Some men feel it is alright to neglect basic hygiene out of sheer laziness, but a woman will never go out with you again if you show up at her home with body odor or dirty fingernails. Imagine you are out with the girl of your dreams. How do you think she is going to react when you go in for that first kiss and you have not brushed your teeth in days? Whether you are planning to go out on a date or not, it is disgusting to leave your home in such a condition. Brush your hair and teeth, trim your nails, and make sure all unwanted hair is kept at bay.

Chapter 2: Preparing for the Approach

Before you start thinking about approaching women, you need to know exactly what type of woman you are interested in. Imagine the woman of your dreams. How does she look? What kind of music does she like? What type of personality does she have? Do you prefer a sweet woman, or are you drawn to someone with a more sarcastic and biting demeanor? Imagine every detail. Have fun with this exercise.

Now that you have a picture of your dream woman in mind, you will approach women differently. When you know what you are looking for, you undoubtedly will attract it. When meeting a woman for the first time, you will be able to figure out pretty quickly if she is the one for you. Walk up to her and get to know her. Ask her questions to see if she aligns with what you are looking for. If she does not measure up exactly, that is alright. If you were attracted to her, she must share some of the characteristics you were looking for. Ask her questions based on the qualities that are important to you. If you are looking for a smart girl, ask her questions to test her intelligence. If you are looking for someone sporty, find out what activities she likes to participate in. If you would like to find someone with a keen sense of adventure, talk about the different trips you have taken. Once you know what you are looking for, you will not simply settle on the first girl who accepts your invitation. Knowing what you want makes you more attractive to the opposite sex.

When you want to approach a woman, keep in mind that every woman is unique. What may have worked with one woman might not necessarily work on another.

Be confident when you make your approach. Women are drawn to men with a strong sense of self-confidence. Stand with your head held high. Even if you feel like this woman is "out of your league", you need to realize there is simply no such thing. With an air of confidence and your own personal style, you will be able to start a conversation with any woman you meet.

Do not get hung up on the kind of car you drive or the job you currently hold. It is not worth it to be with a woman who refuses you because of the brands you wear or the model of your vehicle. These types of women are very superficial and phony. They do not make good girlfriends — or good wives, for that matter. Even if a woman has high expectations, she will still appreciate a man who proves that he has what it takes. She will fall for a good man who has confidence, style, and good manners.

Always be yourself. Stay true to your own beliefs, dreams, and sense of style. Talk to women with confidence, and you will earn their respect (and possibly a date). Do not use words like "maybe" when asking out a woman. Have enough confidence in yourself to clearly state your intentions. What is the worst thing that could happen if you put yourself out there? The woman can say "no." That is not really a loss, considering how many more women there are out there. You should not count this rejection as a loss, because these women were never really yours to begin with and you are not entitled to their yeses.

Chapter 3: Starting a Conversation

When you spot a beautiful woman, avoid falling for the lure to use a pick up line. You don't want her first impression of you to include 'unoriginal' and 'corny' so be ready with a better conversation starter. In some cases, you can ask a woman for directions, or pretend you do not know how to do something. This can possibly buy you a few minutes, but the conversation needs to progress from there. If you cannot come up with a way to keep the conversation going, she will probably politely smile and make a quick exit.

You can start off with a joke or simply find a way to make her smile. Try to make your first conversation last for about five minutes. If you can keep her interested and engaged for five minutes or more, you are almost guaranteed to get her phone number and possibly that first date.

When initiating a conversation, try to keep the following points in mind:

Confidence Level – A woman will be able to sense your level of confidence when you are standing in front of her. If you exude confidence, your chances of landing that first date will be greater.

Tone – Your vocal inflections will clue her in to the fact that you are nervous. Keep your tone strong and steady.

Appearance – Make sure you have taken care of all your personal hygiene needs before approaching her. If you have not brushed your hair or teeth, or have skimped on deodorant, you will have little to no chance with her.

Sense of Humor – Women love men who can make them laugh.

Eye Contact – Show you are interested in what she is saying by keeping good eye contact with her. Also, do not let your gaze turn to her chest. If she finds you staring at her cleavage, she will find most likely find that disrespectful, and you will have absolutely no chance with her.

Body Language – Keep calm and relaxed. A woman can sense when you are tense, and this may make her uneasy.

How to Keep the Conversation Going:

Sure, women love men with a great sense of humor. You reel them in with a few great jokes and keep them laughing all night long. Women love to hang out with funny men, but after time, jokes can start to become tedious and boring. If all you are feeding her are jokes, she will probably lose interest pretty quickly. If all she is hearing are funny stories and nothing else, she is going to feel like you have nothing important to say.

Create meaningful conversation. Ask her about her likes and dislikes. Get to know what makes her happy; what she cares about. Ask her how she spends her day, what her dreams are. Throw in a few funny jokes here and there, but make sure you work also at connecting with her on a deeper level. Notice the small details and prove yourself to be a good observer when it comes to her and what she has to say. Most women find that a great conversationalist is the perfect match for them.

During your conversation, take notice of her body language as well. Pay attention to her gestures. How is she responding to you? What is she saying? How does she look at you? If you find that she is becoming bored with your conversation, quickly adapt and lead the conversation to a different topic. Ask her another question about herself and get her talking about something new. Do not keep the conversation revolving around you. Get her to talk about herself as well. Pay attention to her and listen well. By doing this, you will gain a better understanding of her, and women always appreciate a good listener.

Important Note: Do Not Look at Other Women When You Are Hanging Out

Even if you have just met this woman, it is disrespectful to be checking out other women when you are getting to know one another. Yes, you may be single, but if you ever want to find that special someone, you need to know how to treat a woman right. Checking out another woman's backside or chest will make for a very uncomfortable situation.

Chapter 4: Using the Internet to Your Advantage

A large part of our social lives have moved in a more virtual direction, due to the rise of social media. Many relationships start and develop through social media. The internet helps us to stay connected to each other through e-mails and various social networks.

Many men scope out women through internet dating sites or on social media. If you are open to using dating sites, these sites can help you meet new people who match certain preferences you can specify, like location, interests, etc. You may be able to connect with a girl through mutual friends on Facebook. It may be someone you know casually, or maybe have met at a party. Through looking at photographs on her Facebook profile, you can get a sense of what kind of person she is. You can see how she interacts with other men and women online.

If you get to know her online first, you will be at an advantage. You can get to know her interests and favorite things better, so that once you start connecting you will be able to easily impress her.

You can use social media to take that first step. You can send her a message and get the conversation started. Sometimes, it can be easier to chat online and then carry on the conversation face to face if all goes.

If this woman has been your online friend for weeks, months, or years, it should be easier to build a relationship with her. Chances are she already knows your basic character. If she likes what she has seen so far, she has already decided the type of man you are.

Show a genuine interest in what is important for her. Leave a kind comment on her posts and photos and try to connect with her through various Facebook groups and pages. If you like similar things, then conversation starters will come easily to you. Check out what her hobbies are and see if they correlate with yours.

Ways to Break the Ice Online:

- Tell her that it has been a long time since you spoke and you would love to reconnect with her again. This only works if you know her outside the internet.

- Compliment her photos. Tell her she looks beautiful in her new profile picture. Compliments can go a long way toward bringing an online relationship offline. However, remember to be sincere with your compliments. Try not to lay it on too thick.

- Get her talking about her favorite movies, actors, artists, or musical groups. Try to find some common ground.

- If you are feeling confident that she is showing an interest in you as well, ask her to meet casually for a cup of coffee at the local coffee shop. Let her know that you would really like to get to know her better.

- Stay in contact with her. If she is genuinely someone you would like to get to know better and form a relationship with, be there for her. Even if she does not become a romantic partner, you will always have a friend in her.

What to Avoid:

- Do not rush into anything. Starting with a meet-up is never a good idea. Develop the relationship online first. Get to know her first and develop a relationship of mutual fondness. Securing her phone number is a good indicator that you have established enough trust between you to give out personal information. Only then can you can ask her on date.

- Be respectful. Although you will have access to a lot of personal information about her through your connection on social media, respect her privacy. Do not ask or comment about personal things you read on her profiles, beyond what is accepted as polite. Do not ask about her previous relationships and family history (Save these questions for after you have met her a few times). Do not talk about her breasts or her butt. You may easily turn off a woman with this type of talk. Worse, if she is a woman you only know casually online, she will think you are some sort of pervert.

- Never come on to her sexually online. That just makes you look like a jerk. Prepare to be unfriended and/or blocked.

- Do not monopolize the conversation by talking about yourself. Show a genuine interest in her life, work, and hobbies.

- Never question her about the other men she talks to online. If she is not in a relationship with you, you do not have a right to ask. Also, chatting with other men is not cheating, even if you were in a relationship. Jealously is not an appealing quality in a man.

Chapter 5: Planning an Unforgettable First Date

After you have a successful conversation to break the ice, you may feel confident enough to ask this woman on a date. Put some time and effort into planning a day she will remember. Try to mesh multiple "dates" into one date to round off the whole experience nicely. Take her out to dinner, then go to the movies, followed by coffee and dessert at a local cafe. By structuring your date in this way, you are creating three separate experiences from which to draw fond memories.

It's the little things that show you are attentive and caring that will make your night out memorable. Always aim to impress her with your full attention during your initial dates and thereafter. Here are a few ways to make sure you leave a good impression:

- Be punctual when setting a time and a place to meet. If you are picking her up at her place for a date, make sure you are on time. Never keep a date waiting.

- Be a gentleman at all times. Simply follow the rules of good manners. Treat her as you would expect your sister, mother, or grandmother to be treated.

- Go out of your way to make her feel good about herself. Your date would have put effort to make herself pretty for the occasion. Be vocal with what you like about her appearance, in a sincere and respectful way. Compliment her outfit or her shoes. Tell her she looks beautiful.

- Always be polite. Treat her and all those close to her with the utmost respect and kindness.

- Surprise her with flowers or small gifts. Sometimes, these surprises do not need to be bought. You do not always need to take her out to fancy restaurants. Little things can go a long way to make her happy.

- Always be honest with her.

- Be chivalrous. Helping her with her coat, pulling out her chair, or opening the car door for her are all great old-school ways to show a woman she is important to you. These displays are not always common these days, so these acts will help you to stand out from the crowd.

- Be confident in your ability to easily fit into her network. Women are attracted to social men. Engage her friends and family in conversation. If you impress people important to her, you will surely impress her as well.

- Never take a call or check a text in the middle of a conversation. The ability to ignore your phone is one of the simplest ways to impress a woman. Too many people think it is acceptable to check their phone when out on a date. A woman deserves all of your attention, so if you want to impress her, silence your phone or else turn it off completely when you are with her. Prove to her that she has your undivided attention.

- Ask for her advice when you are making a decision. Bring her along when you are shopping for a new piece of furniture or appliance. Show her that you value her opinion.

- Always be reliable. If you say you are going to call her, make sure you call. If she needs your help with a home-improvement project, show up with your tools. If her car breaks down, pick her up. Make sure she knows she can always depend on you.

- Make her a priority. If you have plans to go to her place to watch a movie and your friends call to see if you want to go watch the game, do not blow off your girlfriend to hang out with your friends. When trying to impress a woman, make sure she knows she comes first in your life.

- Most importantly, never force a woman to do anything she does not feel comfortable with.

Chapter 6: Advancing to a Relationship

Once you have made it past the first date, you need to work on nurturing your relationship. This will take time and patience. A good relationship does not grow overnight. With plenty of hard work, open communication and understanding, your relationship will mature and progress.

So, you've been out on a few dates and you are ready to make a commitment. Now what?

Call often and schedule more dates. Introduce her to your family and show an interest in meeting her family too. Bring her to family events. Make sure she knows you are invested in this relationship.

Do not rush into becoming intimate. Start off slowly with hand-holding and kissing. Give the relationship time to develop.

Talk about your wants and needs. Tell her your dreams and where you see yourself in the future. Ask her where she sees herself a few years down the line. Open up to each other about your feelings. Continue to spend more time together strengthening your relationship.

The foundation of a strong relationship is based in the mutual love and respect that develops overtime. If you go into the relationship, with ulterior motives, such as money or sex, you are cheating yourself out of the opportunity to possibly develop something deeper.

A lasting relationship starts with a basic compatibility test. Work together to answer the following questions to get a better idea of where your relationship is headed:

- What importance do your careers play in your lives?

- Do either of you expect needing to move away in order to expand your career? Is your partner ready and/or open to that possibility?

- What are your five and ten-year goals? Can you achieve these goals and still have time for a serious relationship?

- What is your ideal family? Everyone grows up with a different family dynamic. Do you come from similar backgrounds, or do you need to work to understand your partner's frame of reference?

- Are you open to having children? If so, how many? When?

- What type of lifestyle do you imagine together? Is this sustainable based on your goals for your career and family?

Remember, life is full of change. There is an old Yiddish saying that goes like this: "Man plans, God laughs." Suddenly and unexpectedly, your life and relationship will always change. Are you ready and willing to respond in unison, or does every deviation cause a severe argument?

If you find that you are unable to work through challenges, it is likely your new love has personal priorities that are not in sync with yours. There will always be some issues where you may be willing to yield, so look at working out a compromise. In the end you need to be true to the person you are and want to become.

Just like when you first met her, she will respect your confidence and appreciate the goals you have set for yourself. Ultimately, if you are always giving in all the time, you will not have a balanced and healthy relationship that can stand the test of time.

Conclusion

When approaching a beautiful woman, make sure you always stay true to yourself. When you have good self-esteem and remember that you will bring value to a relationship, you will exude confidence. When you are sure of yourself and speak with confidence, you will earn a woman's respect.

When looking to attain a new and lasting relationship, you must:

- Get a picture in your mind of what type of woman you are looking for.
- Make sure you are presenting the best "you" that you can.
- Have confidence in yourself and your abilities.
- Treat women with respect at all times.
- Be open and honest in all areas of your life and relationships.
- Take things slowly.

If your woman feels acknowledged and valued, if you sincerely care for her, then she will want to be with you. She will try to be the woman of your dreams, and you will be on your way. Good luck!

Finally, I'd like to thank you for purchasing this book! If you enjoyed it or found it helpful, I'd greatly appreciate it if you'd take a moment to leave a review on Amazon. Thank you!

Printed in Great Britain
by Amazon